FLYING FREIGHTERS

FLYING FREIGHTERS

JOHN K. MORTON

CARGO

SU-GAC
AIRBUS A300

Airlife
England

First published in the UK in 2001
by Airlife Publishing Ltd

British Library Cataloguing-in-Publication Data
A catalogue record for this book
is available from the British Library

ISBN 1 84037 230 3

Typeset by Rowland Phototypesetting Ltd,
Bury St Edmunds, Suffolk.
Printed in China.

Airlife Publishing Ltd
101 Longden Road, Shrewsbury, SY3 9EB,
England
E-mail: airlife@airlifebooks.com
Website: www.airlifebooks.com

Contents

Introduction

Few books devoted purely to cargo airlines are published and the author hopes *Flying Freighters* will fill the gap that currently exists. The vast majority of colour books on the market glamorise the passenger-carrying fleets of the world's airlines, but one must not forget that a large proportion of the revenues generated by a carrier may come from that airline's cargo-carrying operations. Some airlines are involved only in the transportation of freight, whilst others offer this facility alongside their passenger-carrying flights. There are also instances where airlines operate the Boeing 747 airliner in 'combi' configuration, where the forward section of the aircraft is laid out for passengers and the rear section constructed for the loading of cargo packed on pallets.

There are several success stories to be relayed with regard to some of the companies involved in the cargo business; one that immediately springs to mind is the exceptional growth of Federal Express, which, from its inception in 1972, has transformed its package-carrying business to become the world's largest transport company.

I have received the help of many people whilst obtaining the necessary material to produce this title, and my thanks are extended to each and every one of them. My various trips to Sharjah, United Arab Emirates were most productive and the fact that airside ramp passes were issued to me on each occasion enabled me to obtain many interesting photographs. Thanks are also due to the staff of the UK airlines Air Atlantic and Emerald Airways, together with the staff of various airports I visited, in particular El Paso, Miami and Ostend. And finally, thanks to a very special person on the home front, my wife Margaret, for her understanding and help in checking and proof reading.

JOHN K. MORTON

Air Hong Kong's major shareholder is the airline Cathay Pacific. Freighter operations commenced in the early part of 1988 and were performed by the carrier's only aircraft, a 1971-built Boeing 707, which was later joined by a second aircraft of the same type. The first of the airline's Boeing 747s appeared in summer 1991 and the jumbo is currently the only type of aircraft operated by the airline on its international scheduled cargo services to Europe and Japan. At the time of writing, three examples of the type are in service with Air Hong Kong, leased from parent company Cathay Pacific, all having been converted to freighters following passenger use. B-HMF is the latest 747 to join the airline and was photographed in May 2000 about to depart Manchester.

RIGHT:
A break in the storm clouds allows the sun to appear as Air Hong Kong Boeing 747 B-HMF slowly proceeds to the Manchester Airport freight terminal, following a landing on runway 24R just prior to a heavy downpour in October 1999. The carrier operates a daily service from Hong Kong to this airport.

BELOW:
Whilst having a major stake in the freight-only airline Air Hong Kong, the colony's main carrier Cathay Pacific also operates a comprehensive schedule of cargo flights. Based at Hong Kong, the airline also relies on Boeing 747s to provide the capacity required for its freighter services, and eight of the type are configured for this purpose. Photographed about to apply full power for take-off from Hong Kong Airport in October 1996 is Boeing 747 VR-HUK, a 400 series model built as a freighter with winglets but without the extended upper deck.

China Airlines, the flag-carrier of Taiwan, operates over sixty passenger and cargo routes and the Boeing 747 is used exclusively on the carrier's freight services. Until the turn of the century, five series 200 models were included in the cargo fleet, which will be expanded by up to thirteen series 400 Boeing 747s, their delivery commencing in 2000. B-1864, photographed shortly after vacating the cargo area at Hong Kong–Kai Tak Airport in October 1996 whilst making its way to the departure runway, has since been re-registered B-18751.

Taiwan's second major passenger and cargo airline is Eva Air, a more-recently formed carrier, which started operations in summer 1991. Scheduled cargo flights are provided to a number of world-wide destinations using a mix of McDonnell Douglas MD-11 and recently delivered Boeing 747 series 400 wide-bodied aircraft. Singapore is one of Eva Air's destinations where the carrier's colours can frequently be observed, and B-16109, one of nine cargo-configured MD-11s in the fleet, was photographed about to land at Changi Airport in April 2000.

Founded in 1978, Fast Air Carrier was one of South America's many cargo airlines, and operated from its base in Santiago de Chile, Chile. The airline provided cargo charters throughout North and South America, with a small fleet of Boeing 707s and McDonnell Douglas DC-8 aircraft until November 1998, when it was integrated into Ladeco Airlines, another Santiago de Chile-based carrier and a subsidiary of the country's main airline Lan Chile. When photographed in January 1997, one of five DC-8s carrying the Fast Air mid-eighties-introduced colour scheme was about to land at Miami.

Lan Chile (Linea Aerea Nacional de Chile) is the country's national airline, which was founded by the Chilean government and established in 1929 as Linea Aéropostal Santiago-Arica. The title Lan Chile was adopted in 1932. The airline has a major shareholding in Ladeco, into which the carrier Fast Air was integrated. Lan Chile's operations include scheduled international, domestic and regional passenger services together with cargo operations to a large number of destinations throughout the Americas. Newly delivered Boeing 767s configured purely for cargo operation supplement the last remaining McDonnell Douglas DC-8 in the freighter fleet of the airline, and Boeing twin-jet 767 CC-CZZ is seen here about to enter the cargo-ramp area at Miami in December 1999.

LEFT AND ABOVE:
LAB Airlines (Lloyd Aereo Boliviano) is a long-established scheduled passenger and cargo airline and one of the oldest airlines in the world, having been in business since 1925. The majority of the airline's fleet are passenger-configured, but one aircraft, a 1968-built Boeing 707, has provided the carrier's freight services since being introduced to the airline in summer 1981 following conversion from passenger-carrying use, formerly in service with American Airlines. Now registered CP-1698, the classic jetliner was making one of its regular flights into Miami when photographed in January 1998 during the unloading of its pallet-loaded cargo.

RIGHT:
Starting in 1977 as a subsidiary of Germany's national airline Lufthansa, German Cargo Services eventually operated a varied fleet of Boeing 737s, 747s and McDonnell Douglas DC-8s on flights originating from its Frankfurt base, until it was renamed Lufthansa Cargo Airlines in 1994. Whilst bearing the carrier's original titles, Boeing 747 series 200 D-ABYY was photographed in August 1993 shortly after leaving the Frankfurt/Main freight terminal.

BELOW:
Lufthansa Cargo Airlines was later renamed and is now known purely as Lufthansa Cargo. The airline continues to be a subsidiary of the German flag-carrier but operates independently, the first airline in the world to divide its passenger and cargo operations. Airfreight business operates to more than fifty countries with a current fleet of Boeing 747s and McDonnell Douglas MD-11s. D-ALCD is one of fourteen MD-11s carrying the Lufthansa Cargo titles, here seen about to land at Miami in January 1999.

One of Lufthansa Cargo's Boeing 747s had the 'Special Revolution' markings applied at the beginning of 1998, the airliner involved was D-ABZF, which was photographed in April of that year when making one of many frequent visits to Sharjah.

RIGHT:
Canarias Cargo was founded in 1994 and commenced operations in summer 1995 with two leased McDonnell Douglas DC-8s. Flights from the carrier's base in Madrid continued for a further two years until the company ceased operations in 1997. In June of that year, DC-8 EC-GEE was photographed whilst parked at East Midlands Airport. At that time, the airline's fleet had been reduced to just one aircraft.

BELOW:
BAe 146 EC-EPA, seen with TNT titles, is, in fact, operating services for the Madrid-based airline Pan Air, a freight charter airline which commenced operations at the end of 1988, flying throughout Europe, North Africa and the Middle East. Regular night-time freight services are performed on behalf of TNT. Photographed at Liège, Belgium, in June 2000, the aircraft was parked awaiting its next duty.

Accompanying sister-ship Papa Alpha on the Liège parking lot is BAe 146 EC-HJH, also a member of the Pan Air fleet. An alternative colour scheme has been applied together with additional Global Express, Logistics & Mail titles. Both aircraft are in an alliance with the carrier TNT.

Convair CV 580 EC-GHN, photographed on the ramp of Majorca's Palma airport in the colours of the cargo airline DHL in September 1997, is leased to Swiftair, a Madrid-based domestic cargo carrier. This 1953-built aircraft entered service with the Spanish airline in 1996 and operates flights from Spain to destinations in Europe.

Formed in 1972 as Air Bridge Carriers, the airline was renamed in September 1992 and became known as Hunting Cargo Airlines. The main base of the company at that time was at East Midlands Airport, from which scheduled and charter cargo flights were made to a number of European destinations. Boeing 727s, Lockheed Electras and Vickers Merchantman aircraft made up the airline's fleet. One of the Boeings to receive the company titles was EI-HCA, which was photographed in July 1995 whilst operating a service out of Manchester.

By 1995, the Vickers Merchantman had been withdrawn from service and only the Boeing 727s and Lockheed Electras remained in the Hunting Cargo Airlines fleet. Another of the carrier's Boeing 727s made an appearance at Manchester in July 1995 when operating a flight on behalf of TNT, and EI-SKY was photographed upon arrival at the airport, carrying the special Skypak colour scheme together with 'international couriers' titling. Following the acquisition of the airline by a Belgian company in 1998, the carrier was renamed Air Contractors (Ireland), and the company's main base moved to Dublin.

RIGHT:
The majority of, if not all, Boeing 707s in service today appear to operate as freighters, most of them having been converted to cargo configuration following a good number of years transporting passengers safely around the world. One such example is EL-JNS, now flying for the Nairobi-based cargo operator Sky Air Cargo, which commenced operations with this aircraft in 1988. This airliner was delivered to American Airlines when new in 1963, and notwithstanding its age, the 707 looked in immaculate external condition when photographed at Sharjah in April 1998.

Ethiopian Airlines, the national carrier of Ethiopia, operates scheduled services to almost fifty destinations in Europe, Africa, the Middle and Far East, and also undertakes cargo charter flights. The airline was founded by Emperor Haile Selassie in 1945. Three airliners currently fly in cargo configuration, two Lockheed Hercules and one Boeing 757, the latter having operated services since 1990. The aircraft is registered ET-AJS, was constructed as a freighter, and makes regular visits to Ostend Airport, where it was photographed in June 2000.

Atlant-Soyuz, one of many Russian airlines flying the ubiquitous Il-76, was formed in 1993 and is based in Moscow, from which its completely Soviet-built fleet operates. This carrier provides some passenger services but the majority of the airline's fleet are configured for cargo operations with Ilyushins featuring prominently. One of its Il-76s, EW-78801, was being loaded with freight when photographed in April 1998 at Sharjah.

No – this shot has not been included in error! Douglas DC-3 Dakota G-AMPZ is in fact a freight-carrying aircraft and a member of the United Kingdom-based company Atlantic Airlines. Nine of the type are included in the carrier's fleet and are put to work performing cargo-carrying flights and spraying operations. The DC-3 pictured flies regularly to German and Spanish destinations, transporting automotive parts. To celebrate the fiftieth anniversary of the Berlin Airlift in 1998, this DC-3 was chosen to receive the Royal Air Force Transport Command titles and colours, and was photographed in this condition at Coventry Airport, the carrier's base, in May 2000.

The Atlantic Airlines fleet is entirely composed of propeller-driven types of aircraft, with Douglas DC-6s playing an important part in operations. Two of the type have served the carrier since 1987 and are in daily service. In this picture, taken at Coventry in May 2000, 1958-constructed G-APSA was receiving the attention of the servicing team prior to returning to operations.

The Lockheed Electra type also features in the Atlantic Airlines freight-carrying fleet of aircraft and seven examples are currently in service. Whilst all examples flown by the airline were constructed during the early sixties it was not until the latter part of the nineties that they began to appear in the Atlantic Airlines colours. G-LOFB was present at Coventry on the occasion of the author's visit in May 2000, and was photographed whilst being prepared to receive its cargo.

RIGHT:
Emerald Airways is a Liverpool, United Kingdom-based, scheduled and charter airline and has operated since the end of 1987. The company was originally known as Janes Aviation 748 Ltd and was renamed Emerald in 1992 in recognition of the volume of business carried to the Isle of Man and Ireland. The airline's fleet is made up entirely of BAe (HS) 748 twin-prop aircraft, the latest examples having joined the fleet at the end of 1998. G-OSOE currently operates in the colours of Securicor Omega Express. The photographs in this spread of Emerald Airways aircraft were shot at Liverpool Airport in May 2000.

Sister-ship G-BIUV is a member of the fleet carrying the company titles and colours.

Another BAe (HS) 748 to be given a special livery is G-OPFW, which is painted in Parcelforce colours and titles.

RIGHT:
AECA Airlines is an Ecuadorian carrier and operates all-cargo services from Guayaquil and Quito to destinations within the country, and internationally to Miami, Florida. The airline's fleet currently consists of two Boeing 707s, which include HC-BTB, photographed in December 1998 about to land at Miami following a flight from Ecuador.

BELOW:
Haiti Air Freight was a Port au Prince-based cargo carrier and was founded in 1977. When Douglas DC-4 HH-JMA was photographed in January 1989, it was operating a cargo service into Miami. At that time, the carrier's fleet consisted of four airliners, all having since been withdrawn. The company has latterly been leasing aircraft when necessary.

A large number of McDonnell Douglas DC-8s which hitherto have seen years of service transporting passengers around the world, have, like the Boeing 707, now found further employment as cargo aircraft following conversion. One Colombia-based airline to choose the DC-8 for its cargo operations is ATC Airlines (Aero Transcolombiana de Carga), a company which commenced flying in 1993. Currently, the airline is the second-largest cargo-carrier in this South American country, with three DC-8s in service, one being America-registered as N507DC, which was photographed in July 1999 at El Paso, Texas.

ARCA Colombia was, until its demise in January 1997, another of the country's cargo carriers. The airline had been in operation since 1954 from its base in Bogota and was another to choose the McDonnell Douglas DC-8. Photographed in December 1997 whilst parked and out of service at Miami was HK-3125X, which hitherto operated in this all-white scheme. At the time of writing it is the company's intention to restart services.

Tampa (Transportes Aereos Mercantiles Panamericanos), is yet another Colombian scheduled international cargo-carrying airline. Operations commenced in 1973 with the transportation of flowers from Latin America to Miami. The airline specialised in this cargo. At one time the carrier had a mix of Boeing 707s and McDonnell Douglas DC-8s in operation on these services, but the former type have been gradually withdrawn from the fleet, leaving the DC-8s to provide for all operations. These aircraft have been re-engined, are now classified as DC-8-71F and can regularly be seen arriving and departing Miami. It is at this southern Florida city where HK-3786X was shot whilst on final approach in December 1999.

Asiana Airlines is South Korea's second designated carrier, commencing services in December 1988 from a base in Seoul. The airline operates both passenger and freight scheduled flights to twelve countries and has a dedicated fleet of cargo-configured aircraft. The majority are Boeing 747-400 series but also included is one of this manufacturer's 767s, an extended-range model built in 1996 as a pure freighter. This twin-jet, HL7507, was photographed in October 1996, merely two months after delivery to the airline and is here seen negotiating the Macau Airport taxiways prior to departure.

ABOVE:
Korean Air is a privately owned airline and the largest in South Korea. Scheduled, charter, international and domestic passenger services operate to more than seventy cities around the world. Korean Air is also one of the world's major cargo carriers and uses only two types of aircraft to perform these duties, namely McDonnell Douglas MD-11s and Boeing 747s. HL7454 is one of the airline's series 200 jumbos and has flown in the company colours for over twenty years, photographed in August 2000 about to touch down on London Heathrow's northerly runway.

RIGHT:
Boeing 727 HP-1310-DAE is operating in DHL's colours on behalf of the Panamanian airline DHL Aero Express and was photographed in December 1999 on approach to Miami. This subsidiary of DHL Worldwide commenced services in 1996 and the Boeing pictured is the carrier's only aircraft.

Pacific International Airlines is another of Panama's cargo-carrying airlines, currently flying three Boeing 727s. HP-1299PFC joined the airline in the latter part of 1995 after conversion to a freighter following a number of years in passenger service with American Airlines. The company operates flights to Miami where the airliner was photographed at one of this airport's many cargo ramps in December 1995 whilst being prepared for departure.

Nippon Cargo Airlines was established as Japan's first all-cargo airline and commenced operations in 1985 as a subsidiary of the Tokyo-based passenger-carrier All Nippon Airways. Scheduled cargo services performed by the airline's all-Boeing 747 fleet operate to seventeen destinations world-wide. JA8172, photographed in June 2000 upon arrival at Amsterdam Schiphol, has been in service with the airline since the commencement of operations and emerged from the Boeing plant as a pure freighter, being delivered to the airline in 1985.

ABOVE:
Japan's other major passenger-carrier, Japan Airlines, also provides cargo services, its fleet of aircraft identical in type to that of Nippon Cargo Airlines, purely Boeing 747s. The original livery of cargo-configured airliners was the same as that applied to the passenger-carrying fleet, as illustrated by this picture of JAL Cargo Boeing 747 JA8132 at Hong Kong–Kai Tak in October 1996.

BELOW:
Japan Airlines introduced a revised livery to its fleet of freighters in 1996 and this scheme now appears on each of the Boeing 747s in service. The word 'Cargo', originally positioned on the fuselage in the former scheme, is now replaced with the words 'Super Logistics' positioned on a grey base running around the rear metal fuselage. Boeing 747 JA8180 shows off this latest colour scheme, photographed positioning for take-off from Kai Tak Airport in May 1998.

Staf Cargo (Servicios de Transportes Aereos Fueguinos), is an Argentinian airline based in Buenos Aires. The company was formed in 1985 and operates passenger and cargo flights with aircraft leased from other companies as and when required. In order to operate a series of cargo flights during 1999, the company leased McDonnell Douglas MD-11 N276WA, which entered service in the full livery of Staf Cargo. In January 2000, the airliner was photographed operating a cargo flight into Miami, where it is seen at one of the airport's freight terminals.

Cargolux Airlines International has become the largest European scheduled all-cargo airline operating flights around the world. Operations commenced in 1970 and the airline's current fleet totals twelve Boeing 747 series 400 models. Cargolux was the first airline to operate this type in cargo configuration and members of the fleet can be observed at more than forty destinations world-wide whilst performing flights from the carrier's Luxembourg base. Boeing 747-400 LX-GCV, the second of the type to enter service, was caught by the camera when departing Manchester in May 1996.

ABOVE:
This section devoted to North American cargo airlines starts with a photograph taken at Los Angeles in August 1981 of Airborne Express Douglas DC-9 N1285L. This is a series 32 model which originally flew in passenger-configuration for Delta Air Lines before joining Airborne Express in March 1981 and was later re-registered as N901AX. It is interesting in that the airliner still flies for Airborne, one

example of more than seventy of the type in service together with McDonnell Douglas DC-8s and Boeing 767s. The company is based in Wilmington, Ohio, and is purely a cargo-carrier.

BELOW:
With a fleet of almost thirty McDonnell Douglas DC-8s, Air Transport International operates cargo flights on both domestic and international routes. This freighter is

based in Little Rock, Arkansas, and commenced operations in 1979, then known as Interstate Airlines. The current title was adopted in 1988. Air Transport International was purchased by BAX Global in February 1998 and is now a subsidiary of that carrier. Illustrating the ATI colours is one of the airline's McDonnell Douglas DC-8s, photographed in October 1997 whilst parked at Phoenix.

ABOVE:
Originally known as Kalitta, then as American International Airways, this cargo airline has now become a subsidiary of the Kitty Hawk Group and has been renamed yet again, now known as Kitty Hawk International. The company retains its base in Detroit together with its large fleet of McDonnell Douglas DC-8s, Lockheed L1011s and Boeing 747s. Boeing 747 N625PL came into the company fleet on lease following service with Air Hong Kong, which accounts for the overall white scheme carried when photographed in January 1995 at Miami. The jumbo did eventually receive the full American International Airways colours, later being re-registered N709CK.

BELOW:
Sister-ship N701CK displays the full colours of the airline, here seen parked between duties at Miami in January 1995.

During the late 1990s, hardly a day would pass without the arrival or departure of an American International Airways service at Miami, and it was regularly possible to see examples of all three types of equipment in use on the same day. In December 1996, Lockheed L1011 TriStar N105CK was photographed on the Miami cargo ramp awaiting the loading process.

Amerijet International is an all-cargo airline providing scheduled services to various American destinations together with world-wide charter operations. Previously based at Fort Lauderdale, the company moved its main hub to Miami, from which its fleet of a dozen Boeing 727s ferry to and from Central and South America and the Caribbean. The majority of the fleet in service have been converted from passenger-carrying aircraft and N794AJ, the 727 illustrated, is one of only two of the fleet to have had winglets fitted.

This airliner previously flew as a passenger carrier for the former North American budget airline PeoplExpress. When photographed about to depart Miami in December 1998, it had served Amerijet as a freighter since April 1997.

LEFT:
Arrow Air is another of Miami's cargo airlines and has operated since 1947. Scheduled freight services are provided to points in the US, Central and South America, totalling around ninety weekly scheduled flights. During the first few months of 1999, Arrow Air was acquired by the Miami-based cargo airline Fine Air, a company performing similar services. Arrow Air now operates as a subsidiary of the parent organisation, its fleet consisting mainly of McDonnell Douglas DC-8s, of which nine carry the company's colours. One of the type, N802BN, was photographed in December 1999 on approach to Miami.

ABOVE:
The year 1996 saw the delivery to Arrow Air of three wide-bodied Lockheed L1011 TriStars, which greatly increased their capacity as a freight-carrier. All three aircraft came from the Bahrain-based airline Gulf Air, and after conversion for cargo operation, entered service with their new owners. TriStar N308GB was photographed in the Arrow Air colours in January 2000 commencing its take-off roll at Miami.

RIGHT:
Douglas DC-3 Dakotas were still operating regular commercial flights into the new millennium and Miami-based Atlantic Air Cargo's only aircraft was still in revenue-earning service after almost sixty years. N705GB was constructed in 1943 and currently flies cargo on behalf of its company, which was formed in 1994. The classic aircraft was photographed at its base in December 2000.

ABOVE:
Atlas Air is based in Golden, Colorado. Its main activity is leasing out its fleet of Boeing 747s and operating them on behalf of some of the world's leading airlines. Whilst the majority of the aircraft retain the Atlas Air livery when flying for another carrier, there are instances when the lessor's stickers appear on the fuselages, indicating the airline to whom the equipment is being leased. No identification other than Atlas Air appears on Boeing 747 N809MC photographed catching the last rays of the late afternoon sun in January 2000 as it applies full power for take-off at Miami.

LEFT:
Most of Atlas Air's Boeing 747s have joined the company following service with other airlines. N809MC is again seen, this time in the colour scheme of the Luxembourg airline Cargolux, for whom it flew prior to becoming a member of the Atlas Air fleet. Until receiving the full company colours, the airliner operated in this scheme with temporary Atlas Air stickers attached, and is seen in this condition at Miami in December 1996.

ABOVE:
Burlington Air Express operated from its main base in Toledo, Ohio, contracting out its aircraft to other carriers, a service which has been offered since the formation of the company in 1972. In January 1996 when McDonnell Douglas DC-8 N825BX was photographed about to bring cargo into Fort Lauderdale, a further thirteen aircraft of the type together with four Boeing 727s provided similar services. The title Burlington Air Express disappeared during the latter part of 1997 when the airline became known as BAX Global.

BELOW:
Now operating as BAX Global, the airline still provides a similar service to that in operation prior to the name-change, the company's fleet has changed little and its main base remains in Toledo. Three years later, the scene is again Fort Lauderdale where DC-8 N784AL was photographed in January 1999 bearing the revised titles of the renamed airline.

Challenge Air Cargo (CAC) started operations in 1978 under the title Challenge Air Transport with headquarters and a main base in Miami. The airline operated as a scheduled and charter cargo-carrier, its small fleet of jetliners serving more Latin American destinations than any other all-cargo airline in the world. Challenge Air Cargo's first Boeing 757 was put into service in summer 1989 and was followed by a further two of the type in later years. N572CA was the second 757 to be delivered, seen in this photograph arriving at Miami in December 1996.

In summer 1998 CAC put into service the first of what was to become a total of three McDonnell Douglas DC-10 wide-bodied freighters. In June the following year the package-carrier United Parcel Service purchased the assets of CAC and the airline now operates in an alliance with UPS. The original CAC colours can still be seen and have been applied to all three DC-10s. The second example to join the fleet now carries the registration N141WE, and this aircraft was photographed in December 1998 about to turn onto Miami's runway 12 to begin an early morning departure. The DC-10 bears the registration N610TF which it carried prior to receiving its current one.

Capital Cargo International Airlines is an Orlando-based charter cargo airline which commenced operations in spring 1996, providing airport-to-airport transportation. This Floridian company operates a fleet of almost a dozen Boeing 727s in cargo configuration, leased from various leasing companies. N357KP was photographed in June 1999 about to be pushed-back at El Paso, Texas. This particular tri-jet is the oldest aircraft in the Capital Cargo fleet, having been constructed in 1973 and previously flown in passenger configuration by a number of owners including the European airlines Condor and Dan-Air.

This 1959-built Beech G18S is in service with the West Palm Beach, Florida-based airline, Carib-Air Cargo. N697Q joined the carrier in summer 1997 and operates local freight services. The aircraft was photographed in January 2000 as it taxied for departure from Fort Lauderdale.

RIGHT:
Boeing 727 N723JE in the colours of and bearing the titles of Charter America was photographed at Fort Lauderdale in January 1999 when operating for the local company Custom Air Transport. Charter America is a charter-brokerage company which leases out its small fleet of Boeing 727 freighters.

BELOW:
Contract Air Cargo is a small, Michigan-based airline and operates *ad hoc* cargo services and contract charters, mainly for the automobile trade. Its present fleet consists entirely of Convair CV 340s and 580s, although when photographed in January 1997, one Douglas DC-4 was a member of the airline's fleet. This 1945-constructed machine – N4989K, about to depart Fort Lauderdale, no longer flies for the airline.

DHL Airways, together with DHL International, forms the company DHL Worldwide Express, an airline providing scheduled cargo and courier services to cities in over 200 countries. The DHL fleet totals more than 180 aircraft which are seen at most of the world's major airports. The North American Worldwide Express hub is at Cincinnati, Ohio, where most of the carrier's aircraft are based. As is common with cargo-carrying airlines, DHL includes in its fleet McDonnell Douglas DC-8s which have spent their earlier years carrying passengers around the world. One of the type now in service with the carrier is N803DH, here seen about to land at Miami in January 2000.

Another Ohio-based cargo-carrying airline is Emery Worldwide, which commenced operations in 1987, its fleet of aircraft now providing airfreight services to cities throughout the world through a total of more than 560 service centres. In 1989 the company merged with CF Air Freight and this company's logo now appears on the tails of most of its aircraft. Boeing 727 N7638U, seen whilst under repair at Miami in December 1995, illustrates the current Emery livery.

LEFT:
As well as Boeing 727s and three McDonnell Douglas DC-9s, the remaining Emery Worldwide fleet is made up of more than three dozen DC-8s. N791FT was photographed in January 2000 shortly after leaving the Fort Lauderdale freight terminal and making its way to the departure runway. It is interesting to note that the CF logo is missing from the tail although the red and green stripes pause to allow it to be placed in position.

BELOW:
Evergreen International Airlines is a contract freight airline and offers scheduled flights and wet-leasing of its aircraft. One of its main bases is at John F. Kennedy Airport, New York, from which flights originate to cities around the world. One of Evergreen's destinations is Hong Kong and it was at Kai Tak Airport that Boeing 747 N481EV was photographed in October 1996 about to turn onto the departure runway. This aircraft has been converted to a freighter, previously having flown as a passenger version in the colours of Pan Am.

The Evergreen domestic routes are performed by the carrier's fleet of McDonnell Douglas DC-9s, of which the airline has eight examples. N915F is one of two short-fuselage series 15 models that have been in service since 1988. The twin-jet was photographed in October 1997 at Albuquerque, New Mexico, whilst awaiting the attention of the ground crew.

Federal Express is the world's largest transport company and has been in business since 1972. It currently delivers packages and parcels to more than 200 countries around the world. Based in Memphis, Tennessee, the airline's exceptionally large fleet of almost 700 freighters, soon to be increased by a further 300 airliners, are seen regularly at major airports. In summer 1989, the North American airline Flying Tigers merged into Federal Express and its Boeing 747s were given the Federal Express titles and colours soon afterwards. One of these 747s was N639FE, which flew in a temporary scheme for a while and was photographed in that scheme in May 1993 at JFK Airport, New York. The Boeing 747s no longer feature in the carrier's fleet.

RIGHT:
The company's titles have been revised and both airline and company are now known simply as FedEx. Following the removal of the Boeing 747s from the fleet, the airline embarked on a plan of introducing McDonnell Douglas DC-10s, which entered service after conversion to freighters. This type, together with its successor, the MD-11, has continued to be added to the fleet on a regular basis. The current FedEx colours are illustrated in this photograph of DC-10 N319FE taken prior to landing at Miami in January 2000.

BELOW:
A vast number of Boeing 727s flies for FedEx, with over 150 of the type carrying the company's colours. Again, the majority were previously passenger-carrying versions, converted to freighters prior to joining the FedEx fleet. In this photograph, Boeing 727 N218FE is seen about to land at Miami in October 1996. Prior to being converted, this airliner had spent its passenger-carrying career based in Canada, flying in Air Canada colours.

ABOVE:
Another type of aircraft chosen by FedEx is the Airbus Industrie A310 and examples began to appear in the early part of 1995. As with other aircraft types shown in this spread, these airliners came to the airline following conversion to freighters after being taken out of service by various passenger-carrying airlines. This manufacturer's A300 model also features in the carrier's fleet. Illustrated is N447FE, an A310, photographed in October 1997 about to land at Las Vegas.

BELOW:
FedEx uses a fleet of smaller aircraft to provide feeder services from various locations to central depots, where freight is transferred to larger aircraft for onward transmission. A fleet of more than 250 Cessna Caravans performs these duties, and one of the type, N848FE, was photographed about to depart Miami in December 1998.

Fine Air is a 1992-established, Miami-based, all-cargo carrier operating to cities in South and Central America and the Caribbean. Following start-up, the airline's fleet consisted entirely of McDonnell Douglas DC-8s, but in summer 1997 these were joined by a Lockheed L1011 TriStar. The aircraft, N260FA, bears the full colours of the airline and was photographed about to touch down on the Miami runway in January 2000.

LEFT:
Although it had already been flying for a considerable time, McDonnell Douglas DC-8 N508DC joined Fine Air two years after the airline was formed. The aircraft initially commenced revenue-earning service in 1968 transporting Aeromexico passengers, and almost thirty years later, the airliner was still earning its keep when photographed in January 1997 about to depart Miami.

BELOW:
McDonnell Douglas DC-8 N57FB, here seen taxying for take-off at Miami in January 1999, is one of Fine Air's aircraft that has had additional stickers applied indicating that its engines comply with Stage 3 Noise Limits.

RIGHT:
One of North America's more recent start-ups is the cargo-carrier Gemini Air Cargo, which commenced services in late 1996 operating world-wide scheduled cargo flights to destinations in the US, Europe, the Middle and Far East. Six McDonnell Douglas DC-10s were originally put into service and these have since been supplemented by a further five of the type, together with two MD-11s. McDonnell Douglas DC-10 N608GC, photographed in December 1999 whilst on final approach to Miami, is a more recent example of the type to enter service with the airline, having begun to fly for Gemini during the previous July.

BELOW:
IBC Airways is a subsidiary of the Miami-based company International Bonded Couriers and operates freight services from Miami International Airport with a fleet comprising one Cessna and five Fairchild Metros. N811BC is one of the Metros flying the IBC colours, photographed in January 1999 ready to depart the company's Florida base.

Kitty Hawk Air Cargo is a Dallas, Texas-based, international and domestic cargo-carrying airline, having been operational since 1976. The airline's present fleet consists of McDonnell Douglas DC-9s and Boeing 727s. In 1999, however, a small quantity of Convair CV 600 and 640 propeller-driven aircraft were also included, and one of the 640 models, N860FW, was photographed on the Meacham, Texas, ramp in July 1999.

Boeing 727 N255US is one of over forty of
the type operating Kitty Hawk freight
services. This 1968-built airliner received
the Kitty Hawk colours in autumn 1997
following almost thirty years of passenger-
carrying flights, mainly with Northwest
Airlines. The tri-jet was photographed at
El Paso, Texas, in July 1999.

Northwest Airlines is the world's ninth-largest airline, and is mainly involved in the transportation of passengers, although a proportion of its activities involves providing cargo flights to a number of cities world-wide. At the present time, only one type of aircraft in the Northwest fleet is configured for cargo-carrying, ten Boeing 747s being allotted to these duties.

A modified Northwest livery is applied to these aircraft, incorporating 'Cargo' titles. One of the airliners is N630US, which was operating a flight out of Narita Airport, Tokyo, when photographed in April 1999.

BELOW:
Omni Air Express, a Tulsa, Oklahoma-based carrier, at one time had a small fleet of freight-carrying airliners in use on regional and domestic charter cargo flights. Two Boeing 727s configured as pure freighters were part of this fleet, and one example, N180AX, was photographed whilst parked at Wichita, Kansas, in August 1996. The airline has now been renamed and is known as Omni Air International, its freight operations having been discontinued.

RIGHT:
Polar Air Cargo commenced operations in April 1993, providing charter cargo services and added scheduled services during the following year. Throughout the airline's history, only the Boeing 747 has featured in the company's fleet, flying on the carrier's scheduled routes around the world. N741SJ, photographed during the push-back operation prior to departure from Sydney in April 1994, was in fact the first aircraft to be operated by the airline. The Boeing was at that time, part of the fleet of the North American airline Southern Air Transport, which accounts for its logo appearing on the tail.

BELOW:
During subsequent years, Polar Air Cargo enlarged its fleet to what has now become a total of eighteen Boeing 747s comprising both series 100 and 200 models. A new company logo and colours were introduced, illustrated in this shot of N853FT photographed at Miami in January 1997.

Established in 1980 and commencing operations in October 1982 as an unscheduled passenger- and cargo-operator, Renown Aviation currently flies a mix of Convairs and Lockheed Electras in both passenger and freight configuration. The company's main base is at Santa Maria, California, but it is possible to see its equipment at several North American points. Lockheed Electra N356Q, photographed about to depart on a cargo flight from Fort Lauderdale in January 1996, is no longer flying for the airline.

ABOVE:
Southern Air Transport was established in 1947 as an international, regional and domestic charter cargo-carrier. From its main base in Columbus, Ohio, freight services operated to a number of destinations including points in South America. McDonnell Douglas DC-8 N873SJ, photographed about to put down at Miami in January 1993, shared services at the time with Boeing 707s and Lockheed Hercules.

BELOW:
Minor modifications to the Southern Air titles were made during 1994, upon the introduction of Boeing 747s to the carrier's fleet, which continued to be leased to Polar Air Cargo when aircraft were not operating Southern flights. Seen parked at Miami in December 1994 is N740SJ, an airliner originally flying as a freighter in the Japan Air Lines colours. Southern Air discontinued services in September 1998, and restarted during the following year, albeit with a very much reduced fleet.

ABOVE:
Tower Air commenced passenger operations in November 1983, taking over the services provided by Metro International Airways. Based at JFK Airport, New York, the majority of the Tower fleet consisted of passenger-configured Boeing 747s, although three examples had been converted to carry freight. When photographed with wheels almost on the ground at Miami in December 1994, Boeing 747 N493GX was on lease to Tower Air, but was later purchased and re-registered N613FF. In March 2000, the airline entered into Chapter 11 bankruptcy protection and suspended all scheduled operations during the following May.

BELOW:
Trans Continental Airlines operates all-cargo charter flights from its base in Detroit to points in North and South America, a service it has performed since its formation in 1972. When this photograph of McDonnell Douglas DC-8 N187SK was taken in July 1999 at El Paso, Texas, the airline had a fleet of six of the type, operating alongside two Boeing 727s. In March 2000, the airline was renamed Express.net Airlines, the DC-8s were withdrawn from the fleet and replaced by Airbus Industrie A300s.

United Airlines is one of North America's major passenger-carrying airlines and has operated since 1931. Whilst the majority of operations are passenger flights, a small fleet of McDonnell Douglas DC-10s currently provides for the company's freight activities. N1854U, a DC-10 previously flown in passenger configuration for the former UK-based airline Laker, was photographed upon arrival of a cargo flight at Narita Airport, Tokyo, in April 1999.

ABOVE:
UPS (United Parcel Service) was established in 1988 and has become the world's largest package-delivery service, operating 1,500 flights a day to almost 600 domestic and international destinations. A total of over 200 Boeing and McDonnell Douglas aircraft carries the UPS colours, and these colours will soon be applied to Airbus Industrie A300 freighters upon their delivery to the airline. Hong Kong is a major destination for the carrier and it is at the now closed Kai Tak Airport that Boeing 747 N521UP with additional Olympic colours applied, was captured by the camera in May 1998.

LEFT:
The regular UPS colours are shown in this photograph of Boeing 757 N460UP taken at Miami in January 2000. The airline has seventy-six of the type in service, these having been delivered to the airline on a continuous basis since 1987.

Boeing 727 N526PC, resplendent in the new colours of the United States Postal Service, is in fact a member of the fleet of Emery Worldwide Airlines. The company manages air operations for the US Postal Service, providing eighteen 727s for this purpose. The Boeing was photographed whilst parked at Phoenix in October 1997.

RIGHT:
Belgian airline CityBird commenced operations in March 1997 providing low-cost passenger and cargo flights from its base in Brussels. Initially only passenger flights were operated, and it was not until summer 1999 that the company's first cargo flights commenced. Two Airbus Industrie A300s were put into freight service, and one of the type, OO-CTU, was photographed upon approach to Brussels on a very damp and dismal morning in June 2000.

TNT Airways operates a network of scheduled and charter freight services throughout Europe, to more than thirty destinations from its main hub in the Belgian town Liège. Whilst some of the aircraft in the TNT fleet carry the company's own colours and titles, others are contracted out to and operate on behalf of other cargo carriers in the schemes of the companies concerned. Boeing 727 OY-SEW, photographed at Liverpool Airport in May 2000 with Express Worldwide titles, is operating flights for the Danish airline Sterling European.

KLM Royal Dutch Airlines is the major carrier of the Netherlands and was formed in 1919. The main activity of the airline involves the transportation of passengers and the majority of the aircraft wearing the KLM colours are configured for this purpose. A certain number of the airline's Boeing 747s however, are fitted with side cargo-doors, enabling pallet-loaded freight to be loaded into the main cabin, separated from the seating area. Only two aircraft in the carrier's fleet are configured as pure freighters, both Boeing 747 series 200 models, given the additional 'SUD' classification indicating they have been modified with a series 300 stretched upper deck. One of these aircraft is PH-BUH, photographed at Singapore–Changi Airport in March 2000.

The Dutch airline KLM holds a 50% stake in Martinair, the Amsterdam–Schiphol-based scheduled and charter, passenger and cargo airline. The majority of the airline's fleet is devoted to the carrying of passengers, and only three aircraft are configured as freighters: one Boeing 747 and two McDonnell Douglas MD-11s. A regular cargo service is in operation between Amsterdam and Miami, and it is at the Florida city that MD-11 PH-MCW was photographed in January 1999.

Another Dutch airline involved in the transportation of freight is the 1945-formed company Schreiner Airways. During 1999, the airline took delivery of two converted Airbus Industrie A300s, and put them into service on its new cargo routes. One routeing is via Manchester, where PH-SFL was photographed upon touch-down in May 2000.

The second Airbus A300 in the Schreiner Airways fleet completes this spread with a photograph of PH-SFM taken in May 2000 whilst on final approach to Schiphol Airport.

Absa Cargo is a Brazilian airline which has been in operation since 1994. Its current aircraft is a 1966-built McDonnell Douglas DC-8, put into Absa service in summer 1996. This aircraft was originally a series 61 model, and following conversion to a freighter and receiving new engines, it is now classified as a series 71. PP-ABS is a frequent visitor to Miami, where it was photographed in December 1999.

Digex Aero Cargo was one of Brazil's other freight-carrying airlines, formed in 1991 and flying until 1998, when all operations were suspended. The São Paulo-based airline had one Boeing 727 and a McDonnell Douglas DC-8 in its fleet, but up to the termination of services, the airline had only the DC-8 in use. This aircraft was PP-MDF, which was parked out of use when photographed at Miami in December 1998.

The aircraft in the fleet of Moscow-based Elf Air are either pure freighters or combi-configured, and are employed on the carrier's charter, international and domestic services. This airline has been operational since 1991 and currently flies a mix of Yakovlev, Tupolev and Ilyushin Soviet-built aircraft. Photographed in April 1998 whilst operating a flight into Sharjah was Ilyushin Il-18 RA-75811, one of four combi-configured models in the carrier's fleet.

Another of Moscow's freight-carriers is the 1994-formed airline Ilavia. Photographed parked on the Sharjah ramp in April 1998 was RA-76818, one of a total of around a dozen Ilyushin Il-76s in the company's fleet. At that time the airline was involved in freight operations only, but during the following two years, two passenger-carrying Yakovlev Yak-40 aircraft were added to the fleet, whilst the number of Il-76s had been reduced to four.

Titan Air Company is a small Russian cargo-carrying airline and has been in business since 1995. Its present fleet consists of two of the mighty Antonov An-124 freighters, which carry the Titan Cargo colours and titles. Whilst parked and awaiting loading at Sharjah in April 1998, one of the duo was captured by the author's camera. It is interesting to note that the carrying capacity of the An-124 is twice that of the Ilyushin Il-76.

Another Soviet freighter to put the An-124 into service is Ulyanovsk-based Volga-Dnepr Airlines. This airline specialises in the transportation of outsize cargo, and has the largest fleet of this type of aircraft. Photographed on the Sharjah ramp in April 1998, this side-on shot of RA-82078 illustrates the sheer size of these machines.

Volga-Dnepr Airlines has an alliance with the United Kingdom-based carrier Heavy-Lift Cargo Airlines, and small additional titles to that effect are carried below the nose of the aircraft.

Sharjah is the ideal location for the Il-76 enthusiast, where representatives of the type can be observed operating for various companies. RA-76814 is currently a member of the fleet of the Moscow-based cargo-carrier Sukhoi Aviakompania, and the aircraft was receiving attention to its engines when photographed in April 1998.

One of the Il-76s to receive a more colourful livery was RA-76498, which was nicely posed for photography on the occasion of the author's first visit to Sharjah in June 1994. The freighter carries the colours of the now defunct Moscow Airways, a small cargo- and passenger-operator that commenced flying in 1991. The airline continued providing services for a further three years after the picture was taken.

Another small Soviet airline is Airstan, a cargo carrier based in Kazan in the republic of Tatarstan operating services with two Il-76s and an Antonov An-26. RA-76369 is one of the Ilyushins carrying the Airstan titles, and when photographed at Ostend in June 2000, the aircraft had just come to a halt following a flight from the East.

The majority of Russia-based Il-76s carry very simple colour schemes – one could say, 'When you've seen one, you've seen the lot.' There are an incredible number of Soviet airlines and the majority of them appear to utilise the type, merely applying their own design of titles over a white fuselage occasionally bearing a blue cheatline. RA-76783 was in the fleet of the small carrier Aviacon Zitotrans when photographed at Ras al Khaimah in April 1998, but has since left the carrier.

Continuing this series of photographs of
Il-76 freighters, RA-76845, in the company
colours of Mchs Rossii Guap, is seen as it
slows to a halt after landing at Sharjah in
April 1998. This is a relatively new
company, having commenced operations
from a Moscow base in 1995.

ABOVE AND BELOW:
Tyumen Airlines is both a passenger- and cargo-carrier and is based in the West Siberian city bearing the same name. RA-12973 was one of a fleet of nine Antonov An-12s flown by the carrier in cargo configuration when seen at Sharjah in April 1998. However, this aircraft, along with others has since been deleted from the Tyumen Airlines fleet and, at the time of writing, only two appear to be operational.

Egypt's national flag-carrier is Egyptair, the government-owned airline which has been in operation since 1933. The majority of the carrier's fleet is passenger-configured and only three airliners are designated as freighters, one Boeing 707 which has been flying since 1970 and two Airbus Industrie A300s, delivered to the airline in 1982 and 1983. A regular cargo service operates from Cairo to Northern Europe, and Airbus A300 SU-GAC was photographed upon arrival at Ostend Airport in June 2000.

Tristar Air is a 1998-formed, Egyptian cargo airline currently flying just one aircraft, an Airbus Industrie A300. Flights are operated jointly with the Dutch airline Jet Link Holland, which would account for regular appearances of SU-BMZ at Schiphol Airport, where it was photographed in May 2000.

The flag-carrier of Iceland is Icelandair, an airline providing scheduled and charter passenger and cargo operations from its base in Reykjavik. Only two Boeings in the carrier's fleet are configured for cargo use: a 300 series 737 that was originally in passenger use, and a 757 that was constructed as a freighter. The 737-300, TF-FIE, was photographed at Liège in June 2000, sharing ramp space with a line of other freighters from various countries.

Aviateca is the major airline of Guatemala, providing domestic and regional scheduled and charter services in Central America as well as services to North America. At this time the airline does not have cargo-configured aircraft in its fleet but it did operate a freighter when Boeing 737 series 300 N841LF spent a period of eighteen months on lease to the airline. During this time, the aircraft made several visits to Miami and was photographed in December 1993 about to make a departure. This 737 is the same aircraft seen opposite in Icelandair colours and was converted for cargo use in December 1992 prior to receiving the Aviateca colours.

Airbus Industrie A300 N59140, photographed in January 2000 about to leave one of Miami's cargo terminals, carries the ACS titles of the Costa Rican freight airline Air Cargo Services, a company started in 1997 with an operational base in Miami. The airline leases aircraft from various sources, and the A300 illustrated has been leased from JHM Cargo Airlines, a subsidiary of the Costa Rican group TACA.

JHM Cargo Airlines operates cargo flights for other airlines, which include the Salvadorian carrier TACA. The entire JHM fleet is made up of Airbus Industrie A300s, of which four examples are currently in service, three bearing the TACA titles and one carrying the ACS titles. Illustrated is N68142, seen about to depart Miami in January 2000. All four aircraft previously flew for the Italian airline Alitalia.

Uzbekistan Airways was formed from the Aeroflot Uzbekistan Division and now provides scheduled and charter, passenger and cargo services in Europe, Russia and the Far East. The 1992-established airline employs over 16,000 staff and has a large fleet of aircraft totalling almost 100 in number. Freight and passenger flights operate to the UAE, and it is at Sharjah that Antonov An-12 UK 11418 was photographed in April 1998.

ABOVE AND BELOW:
As is the case with the majority of Soviet cargo-carrying airlines, Uzbekistan Airways relies on a number of Ilyushin Il-76s to perform its freight operations, the majority of the aircraft being under ten years old. Il-76 UK 76805, seen with Inter Cargo Service titles, was a visitor to Sharjah in April 1998.

Il-76 UK 76782 was originally a member of the vast Aeroflot fleet prior to being given Uzbekistan Airways titles following the break up of the Aeroflot airline. Shades of the old scheme are still visible in this June 1994 photograph taken on the Sharjah ramp.

The Tashkent Aircraft Production Corporation was founded in 1942 and was the flying division of the Chkalov Tashkent Aircraft Factory. The airline operates cargo services for itself and supplies aircraft for charter cargo flights when required. A new name has been given to the carrier, which is now known as Tapo-Avia, although the services offered are unchanged. Ilyushin Il-76 UK 76844 was carrying the original titles when photographed at Sharjah in April 1998.

Ukraine was established as an independent state in 1918 but was overrun in the same year by Soviet and Polish forces. It was not until 1991 that the country became independent again. The country now has in excess of sixty airlines, and the vast majority of their services are operated by Soviet-built aircraft. One of the airlines that was formed in 1995 is ATI Air Company, a pure freight-carrying airline based in the country's capital Kiev. The carrier's fleet comprises nine Il-76s, including UR-78758, photographed at Sharjah in April 1998. The aircraft is seen carrying the additional titles of Payam Air, an Iranian cargo-carrier to whom the Ilyushin is leased.

Dnepropetrovsk-based Yuzmashavia commenced pure cargo operations in 1996, although prior to this the company provided combined passenger and freight flights with a small fleet of combi-configured Yakovlev Yak-40s. The carrier currently has two Il-76s in its fleet, which saw previous service in the original Aeroflot airline. Photographed whilst parked at Ras al Khaimah, UAE in April 1998 was UR-78786.

Hinduja Cargo Services, one of India's freight-only airlines, was started as a joint venture between the Indian group Hinduja, and the German airline Lufthansa. Only Boeing 727s are operated and all models have been converted from passenger configuration. A regular service operates from India to Sharjah, where Boeing 727 VT-LCI was photographed in April 1998 whilst parked at the Lufthansa Cargo hangar. The airline has now been renamed and is known as Lufthansa Cargo India.

Linea Aerea Mexicana de Carga was formed in 1995 and operated freighter services from its base at Laredo International Airport, Texas. Two Convair freighters flew for the company, a 1954-built series 240, and a 1957-built series 440. The former, XA-TDF, was photographed at El Paso in July 1999 whilst being prepared for departure. The airline suspended operations shortly after this picture was taken.

McDonnell Douglas DC-10 XA-TDC is a freighter that was originally in the fleet of the Mexican airline Taesa. The tri-jet was leased from the carrier and put into cargo-carrying service for the Chilean airline New Southways, commencing August 1998 and continuing into the early part of 1999. Prior to the subsequent grounding of Taesa and suspension of services, the DC-10 was photographed in January 1999 whilst parked on one of Miami's remote stands.

This attractively liveried McDonnell Douglas DC-8 is the latest aircraft to be put into service by the Mexican cargo airline Mas Air Cargo, and joins an existing Boeing 707. The DC-8 is on lease from the Chilean airline Fast Air, which accounts for the Chilean registration CC-CAX. Originally configured for passenger use, the airliner operated for most of its life in the colours of the American airline United Airlines, prior to being converted and re-engined. Now classified as a DC-8-71, the airliner was photographed taxying to the Miami departure runway in December 1998.

At the time of compiling this text the Mexican cargo-carrier Aeromexpress had only one aircraft in its fleet. Boeing 727 N909PG, named *Icaro*, was originally in the fleet of the German airline Hapag Lloyd when delivered new in 1979, and has had several owners during the subsequent years. Aeromexpress put the airliner into service in spring 1997, and it is illustrated here upon approach to Miami in January 1999, following repainting in the company's new colour scheme.

The current Air Cess was founded in 1998 and operates a series of charter passenger and cargo flights from its base in Sharjah, UAE. Only Soviet-built Antonov, Yakovlev and Ilyushin aircraft are flown by the carrier, the latter type being entirely 1960s-built Il-18s. One of this fleet of four is 3D-SBW, photographed in April 1998 parked on the ramp at the company's base. This Il-18 has since been allocated the new registration 3C-KKK.

The two McDonnell Douglas DC-8 freighters in the African International Airways fleet make regular visits to United Kingdom and other European airports. Although it is a Manzini, Swaziland-based carrier, the company's offices are located in the United Kingdom, from where the airline's specialised operations of contract air cargo are managed. One of the DC-8s in service is 3D-ADV, photographed in March 2000 about to depart Stansted Airport.

The Israeli airline El Al has a fleet of all-Boeing products and operates both passenger and cargo flights. Whilst the aircraft put into passenger service carry the full El Al colours and markings, aircraft used on cargo flights can be observed without any indication as to the operator, and bear only the word 'Cargo'. The enthusiast will immediately recognise these aircraft although many examples fly in a totally white scheme. In this instance, Boeing 747 4X-AXF, about to land at Miami in December 1996, carries the company's colours without any additional identification other than the word 'Cargo'.

Boeing 707 5B-DAZ was put into service in summer 1992 by the Cyprus-based airline Avistar, and continued flying for the company until operations ceased in 1998. The cargo-carrier operated only one aircraft during its time in business, and Delta Alpha Zulu, with its quite small titles placed beneath the flight-deck, was photographed upon arrival at Frankfurt/Main in August 1993.

ABOVE:
DAS Air Cargo's main base is at London–Gatwick Airport, from which regular all-cargo services between London and Amsterdam operate to the airline's hubs located in Entebbe, Lagos and Nairobi, together with other cities in Africa. Flights are made with a small fleet of two Boeing 707s and three McDonnell Douglas DC-10s, transporting mainly flowers from Africa to Europe. DC-10 5X-JOE was photographed whilst slowly negotiating the taxiways at Amsterdam's Schiphol Airport prior to take-off in August 1997. This airliner commenced flying in autumn 1993, originally in the colours of Belgian airline SABENA.

BELOW:
Parked and out of service in June 2000 at Ostend Airport, Belgium, was this Boeing 707 bearing the Uganda Airlines cargo titling and motif on the tail.

Sincereways was founded in 1996 and operated cargo services from Kenya's capital city airport Nairobi–Jomo Kenyatta International. One aircraft was configured for freight operations, a 1956-built Douglas DC-6, 5Y-BMM, which was in storage at Opa Locka Airport, Florida, when photographed in January 1998, following the termination of services.

Malaysia Airlines is the Southeast Asian country's national carrier, its main operations being centred around its passenger-carrying flights. As a result, the majority of the large and varied types of aircraft in service with the airline are configured for this purpose. The carrier does however, operate some cargo flights, and a small number of Boeing 737s, 747s and a McDonnell Douglas MD-11 fly in cargo configuration. Boeing 737 series 300 9M-MZB is one of the carrier's freighters, here seen about to enter the Kai Tak runway for departure from Hong Kong in June 1998.

MK Airlines is based in the United Kingdom, and its fleet of six McDonnell Douglas DC-8s and one Boeing 747, all registered in Ghana, operates cargo services to a number of countries which include Belgium. It is at Ostend that DC-8 9G-MKH was photographed in June 2000 whilst departing, following one of its many visits to the town's airport.

Established in 1972 as the national airline of Singapore, Singapore Airlines has become one of the world's most respected airlines, famous for its in-flight services provided by the 'Singapore Girls'. The carrier's main operations involve the transportation of passengers, but a dedicated number of freighters are included in its fleet. The only type of aircraft devoted to Singapore Airlines' freighter operations is the Boeing 747 series 400, and eight are in service. One example is 9V-SFA, photographed in March 2000 after landing at Singapore–Changi Airport.

Index of Aircraft Types

The world's airlines use a variety of aircraft configured for cargo-carrying use. Some aircraft types flown on regular operations are covered in the previous pages. There are instances where airliners were originally constructed for this purpose, whilst others have subsequently been converted for the transportation of freight after many years in passenger-configuration. Below are listed the types of aircraft illustrated in this book.